4-08

OWLS

Tom Jackson

Grolier
an imprint of

www.scholastic.com/librarypublishing

Published 2008 by Grolier
An imprint of Scholastic Library Publishing
Old Sherman Turnpike, Danbury,
Connecticut 06816

For The Brown Reference Group plc
Project Editor: Jolyon Goddard
Copy-editors: Ann Baggaley, Tom Jackson
Picture Researcher: Clare Newman
Designers: Jeni Child, Lynne Ross,
    Sarah Williams
Managing Editor: Bridget Giles

Volume ISBN-13: 978-0-7172-6275-5
Volume ISBN-10: 0-7172-6275-8

**Library of Congress
Cataloging-in-Publication Data**

Nature's children. Set 3.
    p. cm.
Includes bibliographical references and
index.
ISBN 13: 978-0-7172-8082-7
ISBN 10: 0-7172-8082-9
1. Animals--Encyclopedias, Juvenile. 1.
Grolier Educational (Firm)
QL49.N384 2008
590.3--dc22
                        2007031568

Printed and bound in China

PICTURE CREDITS

Front Cover: **Nature PL**: Markus Varesvuo.

Back Cover: **Alamy**: Arco Images; **Nature
PL**: Markus Varesvuo; **Photos.com**;
Shutterstock: Jill Lang.

Nature PL: Philippe Clement 30, Andrew
Cooper 42, Tom Mangelssen 34, Dietmar Nill
37, Kim Taylor 46, Seppo Valjakka 45, Markus
Varesvuo 2–3, 14, 18; **NHPA**: Gerry
Cambridge 41, Stephen Dalton 4, 17;
Shutterstock: Anastazzo 13, FloridaStock
38, Alan Gleichman 33, Dariush M. 21, Brian
McEntire 29, Regien Paassen 5, Jim Parkin
26–27, Johan Swanepoel 6, Brad Thompson
10, Tootles 22, Tim Zurowski 9.

Contents

FACT FILE: Owls

Class	Birds (Aves)
Order	Owls (Strigiformes)
Families	Typical owls (Strigidae) and barn owls (Tytonidae)
Genera	28 genera
Species	About 225 species; 20 species live and breed in North America, including the burrowing owl (*Athene cunicularia*), the great horned owl (*Bubo virginianus*), and the barn owl (*Tyto alba*)
World distribution	Owls occur worldwide except in polar regions
Habitat	Varies with species; many live in woodlands
Distinctive physical characteristics	Very large eyes and a round face; sharp talons; fluffy feathers; some have ear tufts
Habits	Usually solitary when not breeding; most hunt at night, some at dawn and dusk, and a few in daytime; owls cough up pellets made of the fur, bones, and feathers of their prey
Diet	Varies with species but tends to be small animals

Introduction

Owls are easy to recognize with their round head and huge, staring eyes. Many have earlike **tufts** on their heads, too.

Owls usually live alone. Most are active at night, when they hunt. Like eagles and hawks, owls are birds of **prey**—they hunt other animals for food. Owls have sharp hearing and excellent nighttime vision. These stealthy hunters swoop silently onto their prey.

In stories, owls are usually wise characters. Perhaps that's because the rings of feathers around their eyes make them look like they are wearing glasses, much like an old teacher!

The great horned owl is common in both North America and South America.

A southern white-faced owl from South Africa looks out for its favorite foods—large insects and spiders—from a tree.

6

The Owl Family

There are more than 200 **species** of owls in the world. They live just about everywhere on Earth. About 20 species of owls live in North America.

Owls are found in tropical rain forests, deserts, and even on the freezing **tundra** in the far north. The only place that they do not live is the vast ice of the North and South Poles.

People have no trouble identifying an owl. Although they live in so many parts of the world and in such different **habitats**, they all look similar. The features that make owls stand out from other birds are their big eyes and their large rounded head. These distinctive features are enough to group the owls in their own **order** called the Strigiformes (STRI-JEE-FORMZ). Owls still share many features with other birds. They have a beak, feathery body, and wings. Like most other birds, owl bones are hollow, and, therefore, weigh very little.

Fluffy Feathers

Owls have very fluffy feathers, which feel like soft fur to the touch. The feathers cover the bird's whole body from the base of the beak to its clawed toes.

Most owls hunt at night and sleep during the day. They often sleep while perching on a branch out in the open. While perching, the owls stay very still. An owl's fluffy feathers are often a mixture of brown and gray. That coloration helps the bird to stay out of sight. From a distance, the motionless owl looks like part of the tree.

In addition to keeping the owl hidden among its surroundings, its feathers also keep the bird nice and warm. The feathers trap pockets of air between them. The air pockets stop the cold from reaching the bird's skin. Together the feathers and air pockets act like a cozy coat.

Barn owls are the most widespread of all owls. They live on every continent, except Antarctica.

9

The great horned owl is sometimes called the cat owl, due to its striking ear tufts.

Talking Tufts

Several owls have what look like ears sticking out of the top of their head. These feathery tufts are not used for hearing at all, but for "talking owl." When the owl is happy and relaxed, the "ears" lie flat on top of the head, barely poking up at all. However, if the owl gets frightened, the tufts immediately stand up straight. That is a sign to any other animal nearby that the owl is ready to fight if needed.

Sometimes, an owl points its tufts forward slightly. That is the owl's way of saying, "I'm watching you!" When the owl flattens its tufts completely, the bird is saying something quite different: "Please leave me alone!"

Big Eyes

One of the owl's most striking features is its wide, staring eyes. An owl's huge eyes are not best suited for seeing in bright daylight. The eyes work best at night, when there is hardly any light at all. In the dark, the eyes' pupils become very wide, allowing whatever light there is into the eye. The eyes are very sensitive, too. They need only tiny amounts of light to make a picture of their surroundings.

Unlike humans and many other birds, most owls have very poor color vision. The world appears to them in black and white and shades of gray. They are also farsighted. Their eyes are remarkable at seeing small things a long way off. However, things that are close—such as their own feet—are a blur to them. When an owl needs to identify something very close up, it feels it using the sensitive feathers around the base of its beak.

Like most predators, a long-eared owl's eyes face forward.

13

A hawk owl turns its head. Owls can turn their head about 180 degrees in either direction.

Spinning Top

Though their eyes are huge, owls cannot move them up and down or left and right. The eyes are fixed inside the head. Therefore, when an owl wants to look around it has to turn its whole head. That is not a problem for an owl. Underneath its thick, fluffy feathers an owl has a very long flexible neck. The owl can twist its head much farther around than a human can. Some people think that owls can spin their head in a complete circle. They cannot, but they can twist their neck so they are looking directly behind them. Their flexible neck also allows them to lift their head to look upward to a much greater extent than humans can.

Ears Here?

In addition to their eyes, owls use their sensitive hearing to find food in the dark. Their hearing is so finely tuned that they can easily pinpoint the position of a mouse scurrying under snow in complete darkness.

But where are an owl's ears? Owls do not have outer ears poking from their head. Instead their ears are slits on each side of their head. These slits are hidden under the feathers.

Outer ears, like the rounded fleshy flaps sticking out of a human's head, collect sound waves, which the brain then interprets to make meaningful messages. Without outer ears, owls have to collect sounds in a different way. They use the **disk** of feathers around each eye like a satellite dish. The "dish" picks up sounds and directs them into the ear slits. This technique is very effective. The owl can even tilt the feathery disks to track moving sounds, just like a hunting cat swivels its ears to find its prey.

A barn owl uses both its vision and hearing to catch a rat.

A hawk owl swivels
and tilts its head to
hone in on a sound
in the undergrowth.

Lopsided

An owl's two ears are not always identical. Many owls, such as the barn owl, have one ear larger than the other. The owl's larger ear is located slightly higher up the head. This odd, lopsided arrangement helps the owl to use sounds to locate its prey. If the rustle of a vole scampering through the grass is heard by the larger left ear before the smaller right ear, the barn owl knows that the vole is on its left. The owl then twists its head to the left and scans the area with the feathery disks on its face. When the owl hears the rustling in both ears at the same time, it knows the vole is straight ahead.

Silent Swoops

Once an owl has detected prey with its eyes and ears it needs to swoop down and grab it. However, the prey usually has pretty good hearing, too. It will be listening for signs of approaching danger. Most birds make a whooshing noise as they beat their wings, but not owls. Their wings enable them to fly in almost complete silence. The prey will not hear a thing as the owl swoops in for the kill.

An owl's wings are so quiet because of the way they cut through air. A sound is a wave rippling through the air. Big ripples make loud sounds that travel a long way. An owl's wings have velvety feathers with tiny comblike projections covering the front edge. As the air rushes over the wing, it is split into many tiny streams by the feathers' combs. Each stream makes its own ripples, but these are also tiny. Though there are many streams, each one produces only a tiny sound, which is almost impossible to hear.

Owls rarely fly in the rain. Unlike other birds, their feathers are not waterproof.

The sharp talons of a great horned owl give it an excellent grip.

Curling Toes

Owls do not have fingers, so their toes are kept very busy. They are used to cling to perches, grab prey, walk up and down branches, and to carry food while the owl is flying.

An owl's foot has four powerful toes. Each toe has a hooked claw called a **talon**. The talons help the foot grip and snatch prey. The toes can be spread widely to make it easier to catch prey. Three of the toes point forward, and one faces backward. However, the outer toe is flexible enough to point backward as well. Arranging the toes into a front and back pair allows the owl's feet to grip perches very strongly. That is particularly useful when the owl is asleep.

Furry Food

To humans, the meals enjoyed by an owl do not look very tasty. An owl might eat a mouse for its first meal of the day, a gopher for its second meal, and graze on a few moths later in the day. For its last meal of the day, an owl will most likely eat more mice. All their meals are eaten raw. In addition, the owl eats almost everything, including the fur and bones of its prey.

Large owls that live on the edge of woodlands —where there is plenty of room to fly—sometimes kill rabbits. Small owls that live in deserts might have to make do with a few crickets and other insects. Owls—wherever they live—never eat plants. They are purely meat eaters.

Hunting Alone

It is common to see birds flying in large groups, or flocks. Seagulls, pigeons, and sparrows are usually in a flock, often searching for food together. Owls never form flocks. However, a forest with owls calling to one another from all directions is known as a "parliament" of owls.

Owls always hunt alone. If they did work together, owls would certainly find prey more often. However, since most of their prey are small animals, there would not be much food to go around even if the food was shared equally. A lone owl will have to search harder to find food. But once the owl finds a meal, it does not have to share it.

Burrowing owls are active during the day, but hunt mainly at dawn and dusk.

A horned owl scans the distance for prey.

Waiting to Swoop

Owls do not fly around looking for prey. Instead, they sit very still on a perch—waiting, watching, and listening for prey to pass by. Favorite perching sites are a high branch, a fence post, or on the sides of a cliff. In cities, owls will often perch on ledges on the side of tall buildings.

Once an owl locates a suitable victim, it swoops down and pounces on it with its feet. The owl lands with its talons spread open. As it lands, the owl's legs bend and the talons automatically close around the prey. That is usually enough to kill the prey; otherwise a rip from the owl's tough, curved beak will finish it off. The owl might eat its meal then or carry it back to the perch and eat it there.

Down in One

Owls do not pick at their food. If the meal is small enough, an owl will swallow it whole. Larger prey are ripped into chunks, but the owl does not waste time removing the fur and bones.

The owl cannot break down, or digest, its prey's fur, bones, and teeth. Once the food is in the owl's stomach, the bones, fur, and teeth are separated from the rest of the food. The owl then coughs up balls of all the inedible material. These dry, compact balls are called pellets. It is possible to remove all the bones from a coughed-up pellet and rearrange them to make a skeleton. Scientists will often do just that so they can figure out which animals an owl has eaten.

These owl pellets
contain many
beetles' wing cases.

31

Not Always Easy

When there is plenty of food available, owls have no trouble catching enough to fill their belly. However, food is not always plentiful. Owls often have to go hungry. During summer, when the land becomes drier, mice and other **rodents** find it difficult to find enough to eat. Many of them die. The ones that survive spend the hard times in underground **burrows**. Aboveground, an owl has to search much harder to find food. In winter, when snow covers the ground, many of their prey are hibernating for the season. Owls must find what limited prey is available hidden under snow.

Something as common as rain might also make it impossible for an owl to find food. The pitter patter of the raindrops drowns out the noises made by prey. When it rains, the owl can do nothing but wait for better weather.

Snowy owls are the largest birds that live in Arctic regions.

33

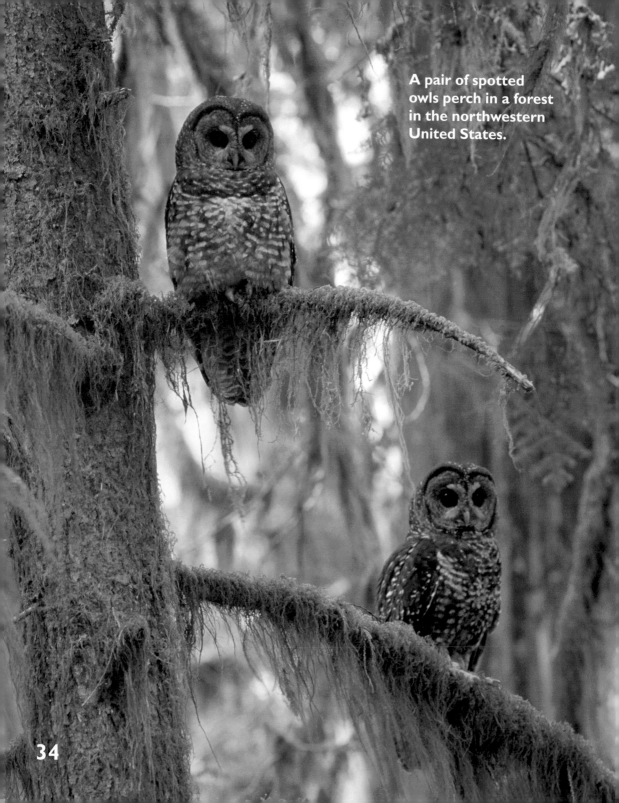

A pair of spotted owls perch in a forest in the northwestern United States.

34

Who's There?

An owl claims an area of forest, meadow, or other piece of land. This area is known as its **territory**, and only the owner is allowed to hunt there. Owls in neighboring territories warn one another to keep out by making loud calls. Many of them call with the familiar hoot: "Tuh wit tuh woo!" Others produce shrill whistles or cackles. Guess what call a screech owl makes?

Owls call to one another late at night. Each owl has a unique call, which the other owls around recognize. The owls know to keep away from one another if they want to stay on good terms with their neighbors.

Hello Mate

In midwinter, male owls begin to call louder and more often. It is now the **mating season**, and the males are hoping to find a female breeding partner. If a male is lucky, a female owl will reply to his calls. The two will call to each other for a while, making a song of hoots and shrieks. The female will then fly off and join her mate.

Female owls are a little bigger than the males, but other than that males and females look very much the same. In fact, when the female mate arrives, the male often tries to drive her out of his territory. The female has to call a long time before the male recognizes her and lets her into his territory. Once united, the male might try to impress his mate by dancing on his perch or performing flying stunts. Male owls might also woo females by offering them a freshly killed mouse. It is worth the effort. Many types of owls mate for life.

A little owl from Spain nuzzles its mate.

Great horned owls usually
use abandoned nests built
by eagles, herons, or crows.

A Nest for Eggs

Owls are good at just about everything, including flying, hearing, and seeing. But when it comes to building nests, owls are not too impressive. In fact, owls never build a nest. Instead, they take over one left behind by another large bird. Some make a home under a pile of rocks or find a hollow in a tree. Despite its name, the burrowing owl does not even make its own home. It moves into dens dug by **prairie dogs**.

Many owls lay their eggs before the end of winter, often when there is still snow on the ground. That means it is harder to keep the eggs warm. However, when the young **hatch** in early spring, there will be plenty of food for them.

Egg Timings

Depending on the type of owl, a female lays between 3 and 12 eggs. If the female was well fed over winter, she usually lays more eggs that year. If it has been a hard winter, she might lay just one egg.

The mother does not lay all the eggs at the same time. She lays one egg, and then waits a couple of days before laying the next egg. She leaves the same length of time between laying each of her eggs. That ensures the eggs do not all hatch at the same time. That would make a lot of work for the mother and father.

Before they hatch, the eggs need to be kept warm, or incubated. That's the mother's job. She sits on the eggs for several weeks. The mother plucks some of the feathers off her belly, so the eggs can directly touch her warm skin. Meanwhile, the father hunts for food for both of them.

Short-eared owls' eggs take 21 to 37 days to hatch.

Tawny owlets from Scotland keep each other warm while waiting for food.

42

Happy Hatchday!

An owl chick is known as an **owlet**. When the owlet hatches, it is largely covered in soft white feathers, called **down**. There are just two bare stripes down its back. The bare stripes are there to help the chick stay warm in chilly weather. The chick snuggles up to its mother, with its bare back pressed against her warm skin.

Owlets are always hungry. They eat a lot for such a small bird and, therefore, grow very fast. The mother stays in the nest until all the eggs have hatched. It is the father's responsibility to find food for the new owlets, as well as for himself and their mother. It is a busy time for the father. He might have to hunt night and day to find enough food for his family.

Fledglings

At the age of three weeks, the owlets begin to fledge their wings. They grow long feathers in place of the fluffy down. By now all the eggs have hatched, and the growing birds need more food. The mother can now leave the nest and help the father find food. She does not stay away long. The owlets might be attacked without her there to protect them. However, as the owlets get older, they grow darker feathers. These feathers help the birds blend in with their surroundings, which keeps them hidden from predators.

If a predator, such as a weasel, comes too close to the nest, the parents swoop down on the intruder with their sharp talons held out in front. When no danger is present, the parents allow the owlets to explore. The young birds might go quite far from the nest. However, their mother and father always know where the owlets are, no matter how far they travel from the nest.

This young Tengmalm's owl from Finland can already catch its own prey.

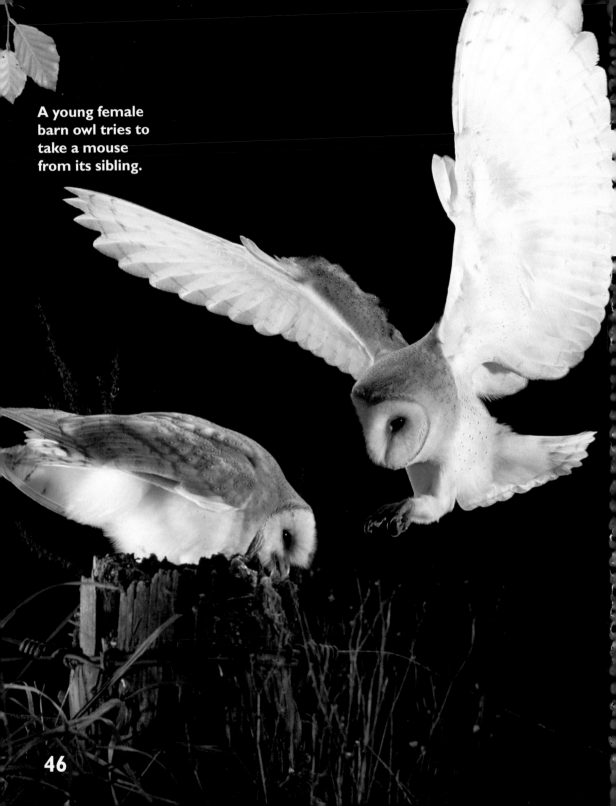

A young female barn owl tries to take a mouse from its sibling.

Spread Their Wings

It takes a lot of practice to learn how to fly. Once the owlets have a full set of wing feathers, their parents begin to encourage them to take to the air. The adults dangle an owlet's meal just beyond its reach, forcing the owlet to flap over to grab it. At first the owlet flutters to the ground. Gradually it gets better at flying, and soon the owlet is ready to leave home and set up its own territory.

The first year of an owl's life is the hardest. It has much to learn and many of the young owls do not make it through their first winter. Those who do survive the first year will have a good chance of living for several years—some more than ten years—and having many owlets of their own.

Who Gives a Hoot?

Owls are not just beautiful and mysterious, they are also very useful. They help farmers by eating many of the rodents and insects that would otherwise damage crops. Without owls killing dozens of mice a day, many places would have much higher numbers of these pesky rodents.

Many types of owls are becoming rare in many places. That is mainly due to loss of habitat or sources of food. For example, the numbers of burrowing owls in several parts of the United States have fallen because of control programs for prairie dogs, the burrowing owl's main source of food. Burrowing owls are now protected in the United States. In addition, there are many owl conservation groups all over the world dedicated to protecting and educating people about these fascinating birds of prey.

Words to Know

Burrows	Holes in the ground dug by animals and used as a home.
Disk	A circle or ring. Owls have a disk of feathers surrounding each eye.
Down	Very soft, fluffy feathers.
Habitats	Places where animals or plants live, such as a grassland or forest.
Hatch	To break out of an egg.
Mating season	The time of year when animals come together to produce young.
Order	A grouping used in classifying animals. An order is smaller than a class, but larger than a family.
Owlet	A baby owl.

Prairie dogs   A type of ground squirrel that lives in burrows under grasslands.

Prey   An animal hunted by another animal for food.

Rodents   Animals with a certain kind of teeth that are especially good for gnawing. Rats, mice, and squirrels are rodents.

Species   The scientific word for animals of the same type that can breed together.

Talon   The claw of a bird.

Territory   An area that an animal lives in and often defends from others.

Tufts   A clump of feathers sticking out on the top of the head.

Tundra   Flat, treeless plains in the Arctic region.

Find Out More

Books

Berger, C. *Owls*. Wild Guide. Mechanicsburg,
Pennsylvania: Stackpole Books, 2005.

Markle, S. *Owls*. Animal Predators. Minneapolis,
Minnesota: Carolrhoda Books, 2004.

Web sites

All About Owls

www.enchantedlearning.com/subjects/birds/info/Owl.shtml
A ton of facts, a quiz, and pictures to print of owls.

Snowy Owl

animals.nationalgeographic.com/animals/birds/snowy-owl.html
Information about the snowy owl.

Index